RICHARD BROWN LETHEM

ROOTS, STONES, & BAGGAGE

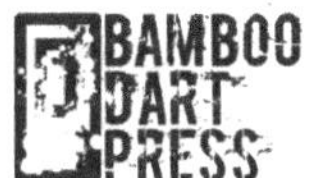

LOS ANGELES † NEW YORK † LONDON † MELBOURNE

Roots, Stones, and Baggage by Richard Brown Lethem

978-1-947240-80-3 Paperback
978-1-947240-81-0 eBook

First Printing 2023

Cover art: "Inspiration (Self Portrait)" 30" x 25" acrylic on linen, 2005
by Richard Brown Lethem

Editing by Dennis Callaci

Layout and design by Mark Givens

For information:

Bamboo Dart Press

chapbooks@bamboodartpress.com

Bamboo Dart Press 038

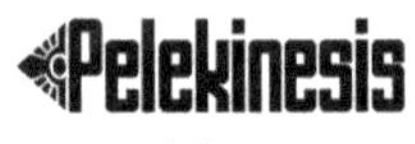

www.pelekinesis.com

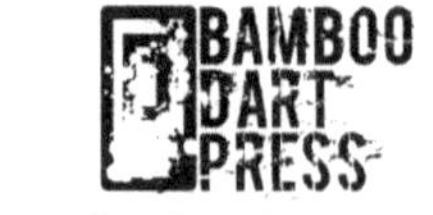

www.bamboodartpress.com

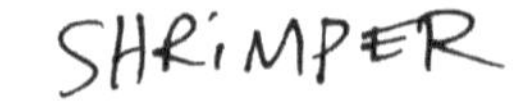

www.shrimperrecords.com

CONTENTS

INTRODUCTION
BY RICHARD BROWN LETHEM

The poet Paul Goodman aptly points out that, as artists, the pleasure of our craft is such joy while the experience we draw upon, the content often is our inner darkness. It is the paradoxical tension between form and content, pleasure and pain, that motivates much of my work. The painting and the writing are attempts to come to terms with my personal experience.

In the '60s Rollo May admonished us to "live in all the rooms of our house." These poems reflect my attempts to do just that.

MY FATHER HAS STARTED A PAINTING

BY JONATHAN LETHEM

"Painters love the winter, they hunker down and begin masterpieces."
– William Parker, *Painters Winter*

I AM TRYING TO ENTER MY FATHER'S STUDIO

I hold four or five memories of my life before Brooklyn, my life in Kansas City, where my parents lived until I was three. These are memories unreconstructed from photographs (there were few photographs taken) or accounts by others.

The one that has seemed certain to be the first – because it is a memory which inhabits a body that is crawling, while the others are those of a toddler up on his feet – involves my mother's arms gently restraining me from behind, as I attempt to enter my father's painting studio.

We lived on the campus of the Kansas City Art Institute, the college where my father taught, in a large stone building with fossils embedded in some of the wall's stones. Being led to trace the fossils' impression with my fingertips is another of the memories. The building has since been razed and replaced.

In the memory there are five or six steps to my father's studio's door. It feels attainable.

At other times I will be invited to enter. Photographs show this: a toddler standing propped on the studio's wall, with a crayon in hand, scribbling beside the father painting. But this is a photograph, not a memory.

Not now. This is not the time. He needs to be alone now to paint.

I AM A FUNCTION OF MY FATHER'S STUDIO

In Brooklyn, for fifteen years or so, my coming of age partly involved a negotiation of my proximity from the scene of my father's painting. My entry into that space was always charged. Not because he required imperial solitude – a requirement, in that family, in that house, in that city, in those years, that would have been met with an absurd, almost gleeful refusal by the oceans of reality that battered at his studio door – but because it meant so much for me to enter.

I painted and drew. In his studio beside him, and elsewhere. I sat for a portrait, five or six times, and sat watching as he painted my mother, my siblings, others. I stood before his canvases and spoke with him about the results, the impasses, the connections. I sat and read while he painted. Once, I snuck in and altered, on a canvas not yet dry, a few brushstrokes that bothered me. I sat in groups of artists including my father and drew from the nude models they'd hired to pose there. At one point I carved out a space to insist was my own creation, a tiny occupation within his studio: a shallow wooden box of gravel and soil in which I planted miniature cacti and created bonsai landscapes of stones, a strange harbinger of my own future desire for the desert.

Then I went away to college, and then I ran away from college to California. Around that same time my father's studio moved to a building under the Manhattan Bridge that was eventually set on fire by its Mafia owners – a Brooklyn story – and for the next fifteen years, more, I was barely present for his life, or he for mine. My place in his studio was wholly glossed in memory.

I AM WRITING ABOUT MY FATHER'S STUDIO

I began to journey back home, and the home to which I'd begun to journey back was in Maine. His studio was a barn beside his ramshackle farmhouse. We recommenced what has begun when in my high school years, standing side by side in front of his paintings, discussing their progresses, frustrations, breakthroughs, and the successions of chapters in his method and style. I'd become witness to so many.

In the early middle of my life, and the late middle of his, I began writing about my father's studio. I did this obliquely, even allegorically, in the manner of a fiction writer, with the predictable misleading results. After I depicted a man in a studio making a painted film, my father recalls being asked, "how is your film coming along?" He had of course never been making a film. I did this as directly as possible, in an essay that began *I learned to think by watching my father paint.* I wrote (somewhat glibly) of joining the groups drawing from the nude models. I added my voice to two or three exhibition catalogs. I was at the openings of his exhibitions again now, as I had been (involuntarily) as a child. Too many to remember exactly: in Maine, in New Hampshire, in Manhattan.

I believe it took my father a year or two not to feel disappointment at my own diversion from the medium of painting to the medium of writing. It took him a while to recognize my writing as a continuation, not an interruption – to understand it as a part of my life that was enclosed in the influence of his practice, as it so obviously was to me. But that time quickly passed. Our conversation standing in front of his paintings (or not standing in front of his paintings) began to include discussions of my own process, my own relation to form, my own aspirations to make things I'd not yet figured out how to make. Some of my most crucial writing depending on answers to questions he'd supply, regarding the life we'd known in Brooklyn, its earliest undercurrents. This remains the case in the most recent work I've done, a novel that will appear later this year.

I have entered his studio, but he has also entered mine.

MY FATHER HAS STARTED A PAINTING

In my father's eighty-eighth year of life, his seventh decade of painting, the story took a turn. In the unvaccinated early months of the Covid years, I drove my father and a few of his belongings from Maine to California. His studio life was collected, necessarily, into my care.

To be clear, collected into a garage. A fortunate garage, one placed deep back from the street, in my vine and vegetable and weed choked backyard, and already cleared and appointed with clean white walls and bright lights. The garage door more or less permanently open to the micro-seasons of the Inland Empire, that hinge we occupy, between ocean and desert. He resumed painting there within weeks, if not days. He remained, remains, a painter who paints. The dailiness of his practice, habituation, addiction, however one might wish to understand it, is almost unfathomable unless glimpsed up close.

Checking the progress in his studio was now as easy as falling out of bed, or specifically strolling from the breakfast table into the backyard. I could do it in robe and slippers, with my morning coffee. After forty-eight years apart, my attention and his studio had been restored to a domestic partnership.

More, still. In deep quarantine mode I'd also shifted my walking desk from my campus office to the same garage, to relieve pressure on the number of remote students and teachers inside the house itself (there were four of us) and to resume my preferred mode of writing-as-daily-trip-to-nowhere. I'm no runner, neither of sprints nor marathons, but when I'm lucky I'm a diligent walker. Some mornings I woke earlier – I wake early, these days – and trudged and moved sentences around out in the garage in the company of his paintings in progress, for hours before he'd appear and begin advancing his own causes. Other days I'd absent-mindedly turn the corner from the house to the garage with my coffee cup balanced on my laptop, thinking I'd be working alone, and find him there stepping back from a canvas to consider the freshest marks he'd made there, and strategize the next.

More than a few times, we simply worked together.

He was almost always happy to find me already there, or to see me appear. Solitude, these days, so often feels boundless. Art, the-companion-of-no-companion, an empty fullness.

Once in a while, though, I'd round that corner and understand that he needed the garage to himself. It happened just the other day. I heard him say, "I'm just getting something going here." I knew the implication, easily, since it called back to that other studio into whose precious solitude I'd sometimes intruded, on the fourth floor of the brownstone in Brooklyn in that impossible family in that impossible city in that impossible time, so unimaginable from the becalmed Inland Empire, lately cloistered in Covid silence. It called back even to my mother's hands adjusting my crawling body backward on the stair and reaching past me to seal his studio door. Yet the favor of my retreat, now, is nothing I can't easily bestow. The weight of longing is gone. This is just part and parcel of living with the old man.

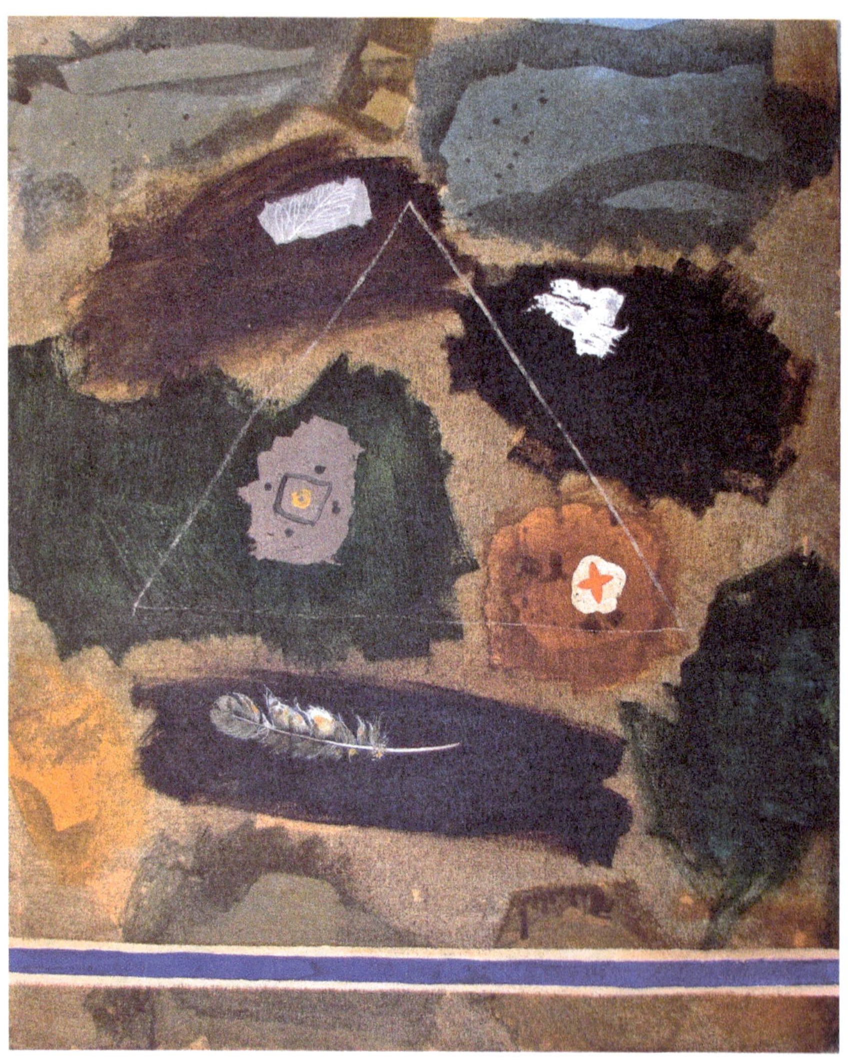

Touch Stones, 2015

IN NEBRASKA

In Nebraska
  many rivers are dry
    this time of year

Have you searched under the orange skin
  with your witching stick
    and a centipede for luck

Underground like a good cry
  a flood complete with roots
    stones and baggage

1970s

FATHER TO SON TO FATHER

Salesman
Nailman
Burning man, where are you?

Your love a sample show
Your curiosity my love can grow
Your generosity the song let go
Your anger a sharp edge to know

The salesman opens the soft trunk made of bottomless secrets, layers of pattern and color kaleidoscope changing to hard layers of steel with wooden handles, tools and guns. Within this trunk there is simultaneously growing a vibrant tree and your hand touches affectionately the branches. The runner stops in the flat landscape to feel his legs and heart vibrating, alone, but being in this special place in body and time is not loneliness but knowing a circle coming full.

1970s

CAUSALITY

Cling, clustered in contaminated space,
the white, the yellow,
Causality is!

Bonded, bottled....the best is the race.
A time or a vertical
Causality was.

I go upstairs—-(ribbon the ribben,rib)
The event is timed. Or time,
more time?

This line or my movement,
completes a right angle
And is countersunk
in substance....

The whole is,
The whole is: piece....a part report,
Invoiced and delivered
by the movement.

I go upstairs (ribbon the rib)
yellow.
Causality is....

1952

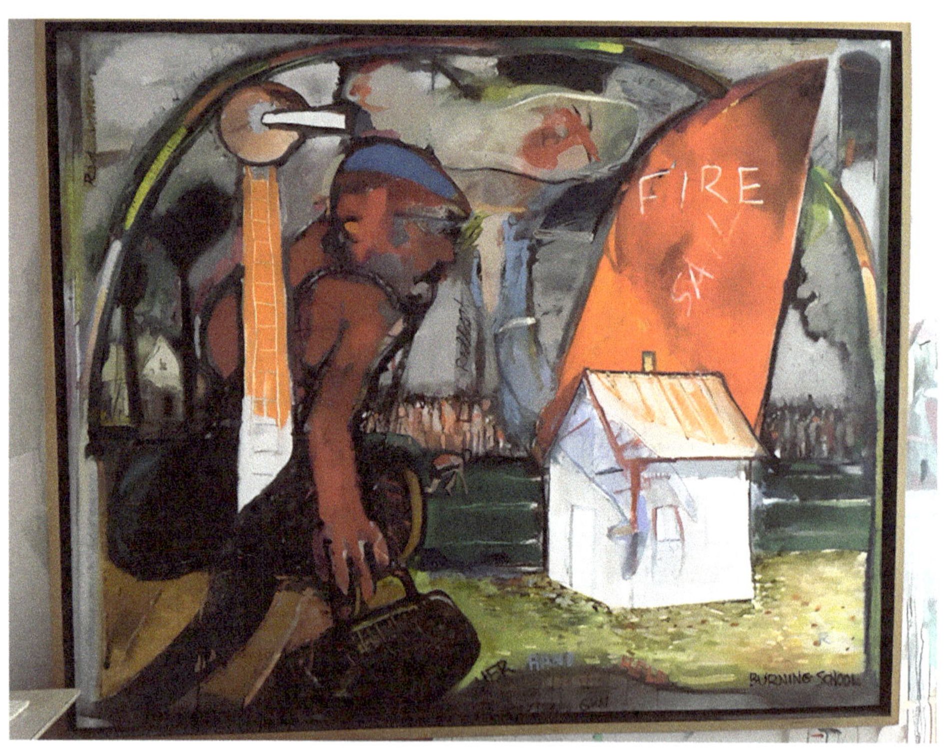

The Compass of Desire, 1994

NEBRASKA CLIMB

In my mother's childhood fears, the sudden spring rains
Flooded the prairie dog river, cutting minor canyons,
Coulees into the clay banks supporting the buffalo grass.
In my childhood a brother and two older boy cousins...I tagged along
Making game where none existed...to scale the vertical wall of earth
Proved a futile challenge, and the dusty thrill of falling
Demonstrated the instability of exposed ground
And the boredom of that Sunday afternoon. Later foolishly
I tried to climb the windmill summit to be
Pried off by my distraught mother.
Another time at five years, I remember clearly the support of the earth
In a joyful spring rain, half swimming, half climbing, sensuous,
My fingers clung to the clay and I called it my brother.

2010

THE BURNING OF RAYMOND GUNN

Thelma and Raymond you have
    conceived me in fear,
My mother terrified, her memory
    of the dust and noise,
Her screams, the lost child
    what comfort to be held sexually,
To ease the weight in father's arms,
    Daddy's gun.
Protect us from the vengeance lord,
    tornado, flood, the unnatural fire.
Who can save us from our passions?
    no one can, so
Yearning, she reached out to him,
    in fear and trembling I was conceived.

1980s

ON BEING IN THE RIGHT COMPANY
(PARIS, AFTER SEEING VAN GOGH FOR THE FIRST TIME)

What makes for fear on the present scene
Is not the new, but the countless repetitions, battles waged
On monotonous plains of little doubt,
Little gain.

See to the realms new sown, after the consuming
Harvest of power.
Not yet vain in the hoping, free of daily hammerlock,
Of common cower, pale sense.

Bittersweet and bruising with unreasoned noise,
A youthful rain on cold, sour January's pain
That preferred not hearing, yet had
No choice.

1960

STONE, STRING, SCISSORS

Of her
Memory is all I am permitted.
It becomes a stone,
I feel its hard smoothness in my pocket.

Of him the memory is a string
Leading down into the subway
It is attached to a stubborn tooth.
It tugs, tangling up inside me.

We didn't find it,
The brown paper bag in the back seat
Of the taxi...unmarked bills.

What I found was the scissors of the storm!
Is that not being chosen?
To walk into the street after the tornado,
Pick up those scissors, work with them until
Sharp and transparent against the stone
They are truly mine.

1980s

APPROACH TO JOY

Satin handed Watteau gives reason to believe
The search renews with each hill top, each consent
A smooth descending through a golden mist
Of elegance which although strange, doesn't lie.

Grand absurdity this lingering hope
Not born of folly but in desperate need
To find the next incline after crest,
Despite a flimsy craft, too much in demand.

And! If all the space is taken?
One must build a raft with what's at hand.
Remember the waters are rough near Cythera
In the darkness many have drowned.

With only the map-like music, often dim
Existing on desire and little else is
A nice trick, but going back, they say, impossible!
What the hell, my mind's made up, I'm going.

1960 Paris

EXILE: FOR OLGA

Foreign spirit, exiled white image passing
On this Spanish turn, pushing aside
The mountains with her snow colored
Baby carriage …tender possessions.

No dream, not lingering either,
I saw her pass alone
Among monumental solitudes.

Myself reaching for you….even
The weighted stone displaced
Could not descend.

1980s

TABLE BEARING INITIALS J F L

Setting out to build a table
I am occupied with thoughts of final function
Then some immediate consideration
To measurement and type of joints
At first, I work blindly
Guided by ingrained sense of horizontal planes
Sandwiched in, four verticles
All tolerant limitations
Such as final platform height
And situation, permanent or moveable
Things needing adjustment, possessing flexibility.
At certain point the shape reveals itself
Combining with a sensuous necessity,
The material feels the need of paint
Or stain or lack of them
Sometime later I realize
It was for you and your poignant affirmation
That this table exists.
That plus the ever present quota of time
And ways of dealing with it
Making strange partner motives.
At my dedication I shall smile
Since I am aware of you both now
It is no surprise when the table stands
Square   defiant   one of a kind
Or that the drawer opens a little foolishly.

1964

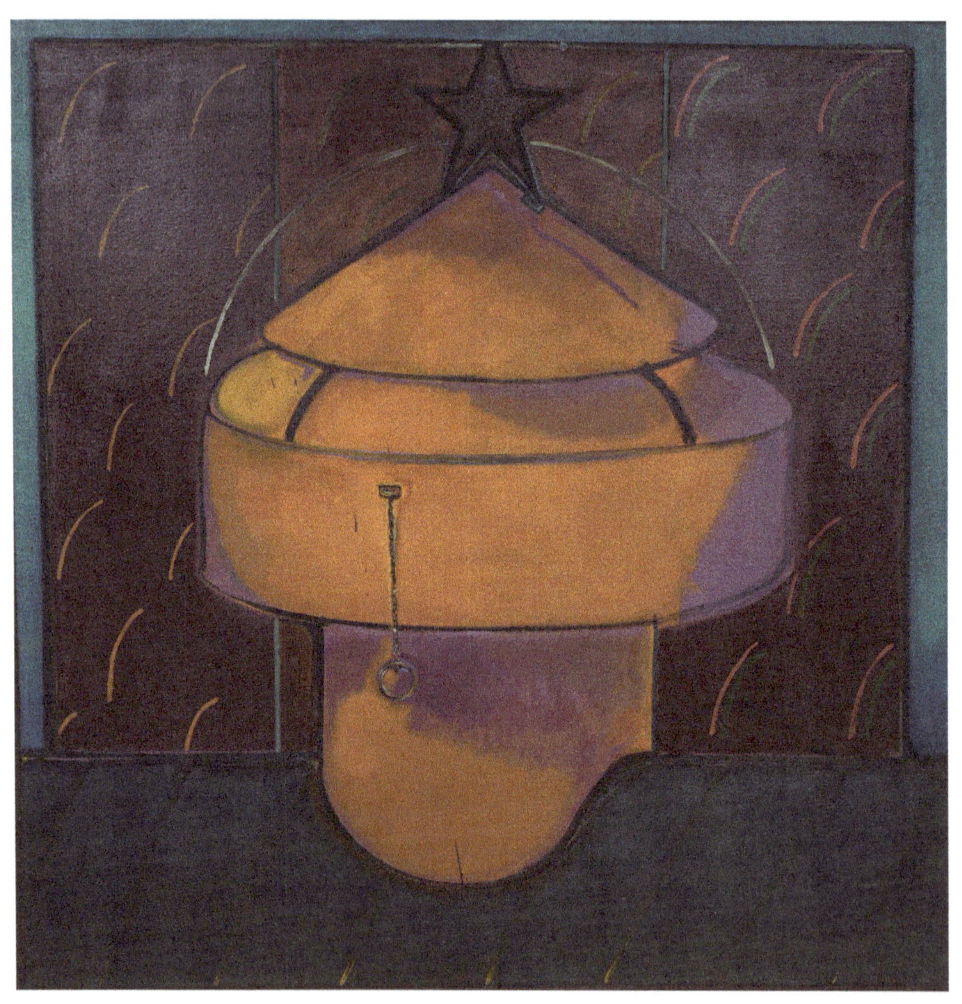

Kansas City Star, 1966

KANSAS CITY STAR : A LIGHT TRIP

Trap/ grasp/

or make attempt to; follow at least that beam of light slapping the

no-colored radiator....bing,,,,bing...bang, up and out over the sill

Glide/

along the asphalt...free and easy until...

Stop/

this is a wild vent...pull chain, dog star peaked

Cut/

light cut like cookie dough by that star leaving us stuck in pattern

shingle under and over...slow going red mica speckled shadow

crossed pattern on flat surface...

Jump/

free...what relief putting eye-arms around box elder...so round, so firm, so fully....

Swish/

right thru the crotch and back forever into pine fringed, void, blue nothing.

1967

HOUSE CARPENTER IN APRIL : LETTER TO FAYE MARIE GIFFORD

We cut a door to sunshine…dust rays finding a garden
And joining Judith's conspiracy , we harbor lady bugs.
I brought you a good one…here in this tack box.

Driving nails into door casing… clean blows finding
Home quickly in the soft pine…scrambled eggs for lunch.
The shell refuses to fall where I think it should.

Yesterday behind the paneling to be rebuilt
I found three pennies, a broken toy pistol, a domino
With three dots…there are always rewards working
Where a child has lived.

God! April is a great month
Always full of thoughts…of you
More than the fact of your birthday now.
This month of gentle warmth…free for the taking
This month of softening earth with its eager
Yellow promises…self fulfilled.
This now you hand me washed and rare

1975

THE ONE LEGGED LOCKSMITH OF HURRY OR GENTRIFICATION

To avoid the fire
    He works by day,
        Our locksmith,

Busy filing the distance
    Between painful events
        Until accommodation sets in.

What fire?
They ask…then bask
In the rosy glow
As sunset at the beach.

Damned hard and cloudy choice, his
To smith the lock secure
Or key the cage open.

1986

IN MEETING

In Meeting there have been oceanic flows
    of spirit…rare but fine,
Sea anemone, gently moving in mindless tide
    tendered by the salt tide's warmth.
More often it is a bathtub feeling
    of body-self slipping into a fluid capsule,
The mind floats free to visions of
    Henry, John, Lilly…..Tom, each
Similarly unburdened, pores open to the silence
    with only the tip of my nose visible,
Calluses soften with memories to that softest
    space that is my possible to flood
With the stuff of God's love surrendered.

I know words will come, as trapped air
    must rise and surface, to break the silence
and rouse the drownded self.

1982

GIVING SELF

Now.....and then in spirit I embrace
Those gathered in seamless unity.
Watts intimates others, few, I touch first hand
Inhabiting at-homeness in the no fear body city
Access to tongues of treasure
Speaking impunity for all
Free at such fine cost.
Born.....we grasp at seamed unities
Our jointing conscious pain.
The shuffled money goes unspent.
God, grant me generosity !

1980s

THE CORPORAL

Hot winds of war and a cold draft
Swept him up like Dorothy.
He awoke in Alabama's pit where hate's dark cloud
Became a bayonet for the unseen enemy.

The enemy he could not find, found him
The sword he slept with cut deep
Severing small parts of soul and name.
He gained weight but became invisible,
Self escaped him in the kakhi camouflage.

Turning up in Texas, tears of desert solitude
Renamed him whole in umber tones rejecting
Ribbons of the corporal, as colors of the coral
Snake to be avoided, a plague of flyover fears.
A future burying the unsuspecting young.

Vision emerged from out the boot of war
Seeds found root in care and kind.
Moist soil engendered light's birthing
To outlast this dogged darkness.
Home calling,
Home at last,
The corporal rests.

2020

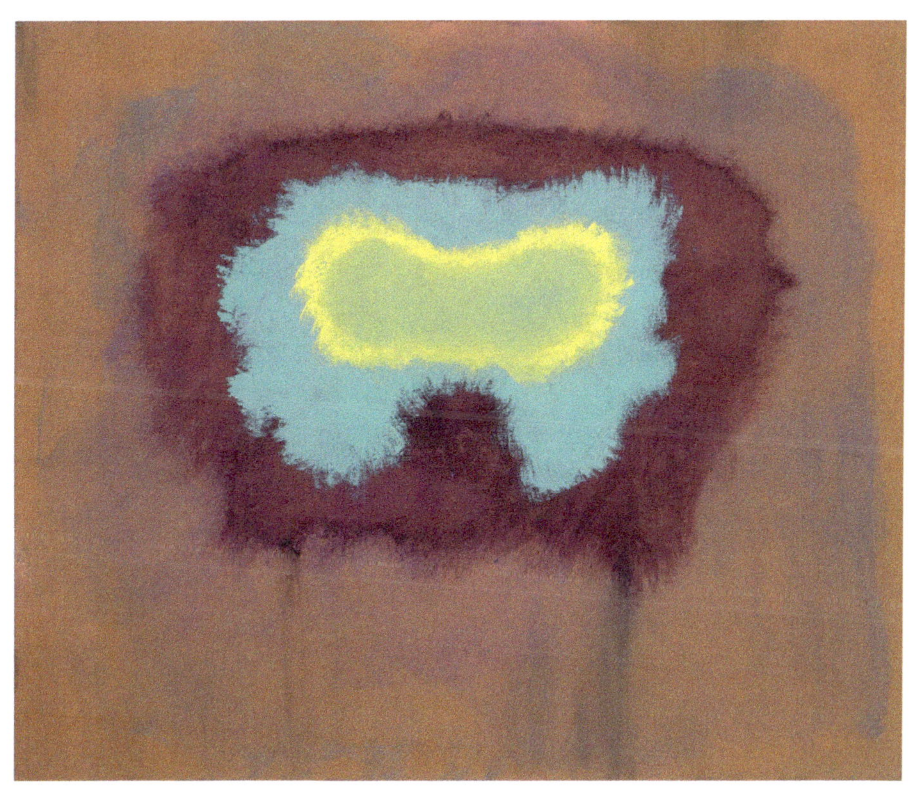

Eye/Mind, 2019

FOR BLAKE

Day of time
    standing still
        under pregnant sun.

High noon leo baby
    at the door of
        life.

You burst forth
    shouting irreverent slogans
        sending forceps flying.

Amazing us with the power
    poetry and protest
        of your lungs.

August 16, 1967

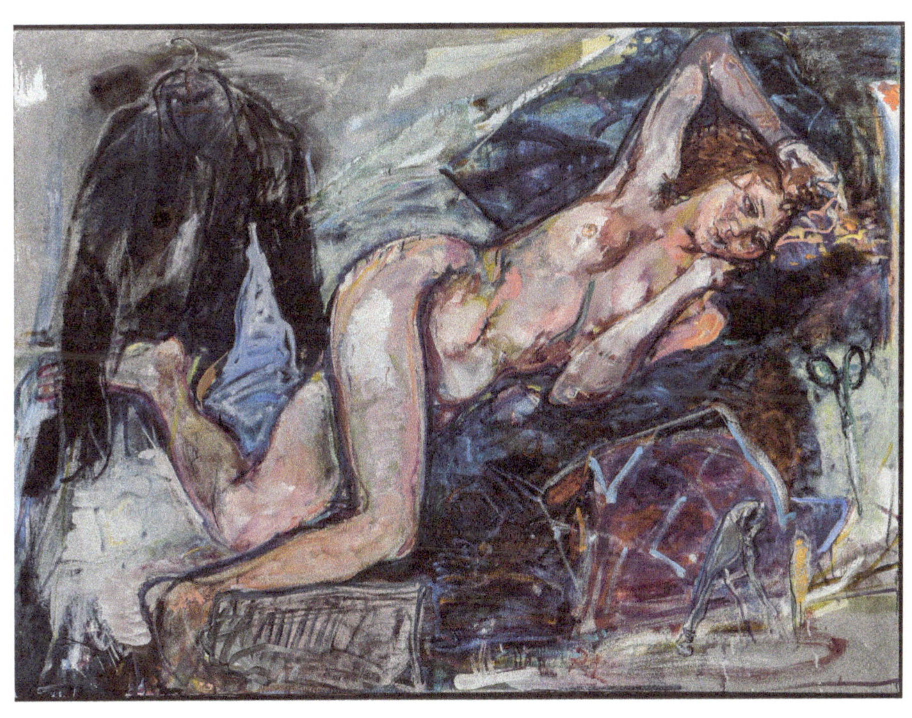

The Woman who Lived Dangerously, 1984

ME AND ISABELLE AND DISTANCE

Now flee!

On red wheels

Of rainbow bred,

Your calm gypsy eyes

Secure,

Where hunters cannot

Reach you,

No matter how we line

The backroads

Of this open season.

1975

ABOUT NOT KNOWING
(AFTER READING STEPHEN CRANE UPSTATE)

Enigma laughing,
        sighing,
              laughing,
Enigma groaning
              with laughter.
Remembering the quiet laughter of children
              the mysterious silence

                                          giggles.

1985

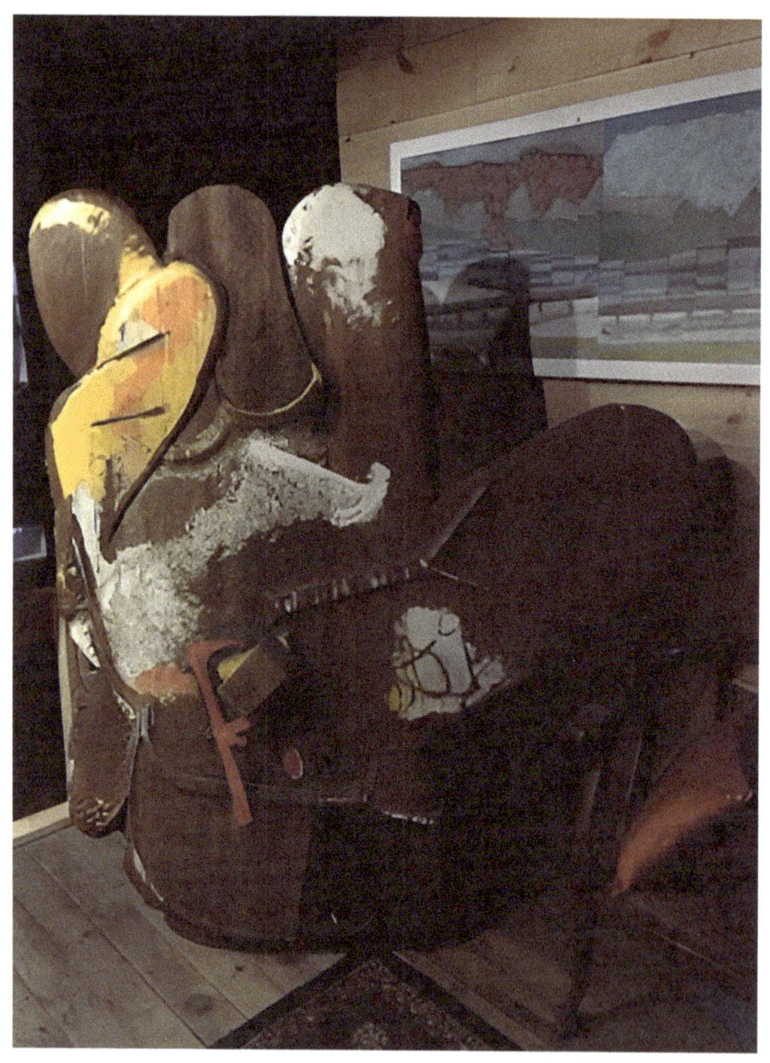

The Glove of Night, 1991

STREET GLOVE

I am the would be patron saint
        Of lost gloves in January
My signal is the glove

Trusted witness and speedy
        Messenger...telling us to stop and look
At what is going down

It signals we are good… and evil,
        lost… and found,
Poison….and sustenance,

Our own nail on which to hang a holy place
        Safe in our wilderness.

1990s

HIKER IN THE NIGHT

Hooded, I am someone you know
Standing in the urine soaked bus stop
Littered with black newsprint,
Everything I own layered inside my head

I am someone you know well,
We have met before in the dark
When heartbeats were audible
What you don't know, is the gesture
Of my inheritance, the direction
In the empty open palm.

1990s

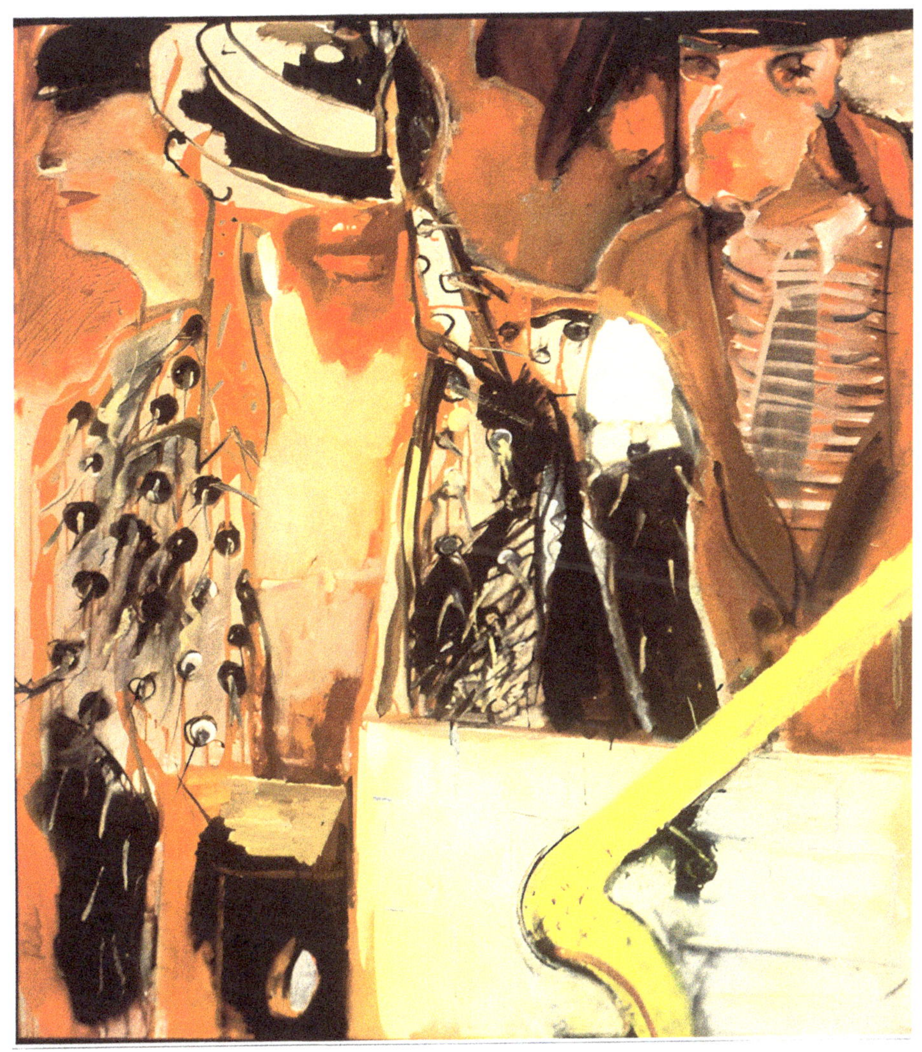

York Street Down, 1989

HITCHHIKING IN THE GLOVE OF NIGHT

Dark night
    dreams of the womb,
        the body wants protection

    the hooded city,   a glove, a shelter
        extend the body into the street

    where ears listen for the love of God
        and ask safe passage.

1990s

HINGE OF HISTORY
(FOR JB)

Passion severe and righteous
Forms the broken ax of violence failed.
No compromise ...but sacrifice
Of sons, home life, comfort, life its self.

Catalyst of change to those in chains
Evil obsessed, crashing into myth and death.
Thy sword John, replaced by words,
Cut more eloquently to marrow bone,
Courage misplaced, compassion lost,
History's hero/martyr...hung.

The just war, recurring confrontation,
Conundrum how best disarm the oppressing foe
Who looks and talks so much like me.

2014

MUD
(OR FOOLISH PLEA IN THE FACE OF APRIL)

My name is wounded tree screaming
In this spring rain, earth rooted place.

The woodpeckers have left me full of holes....like this
The warm wind off the mountain sings and sets me
Vibrating

Still, I stay on this hillside...tho long have reached
And yearned for your fire...and burning.

You console me with these pink blossoms.
In my next life I want to be a wooly sheep.

1980s

DEAN STREET NEWS

The morning news
Fire by death
Intimate relations
Revolver
Waiting for word from the Lord
And steam heat

1969

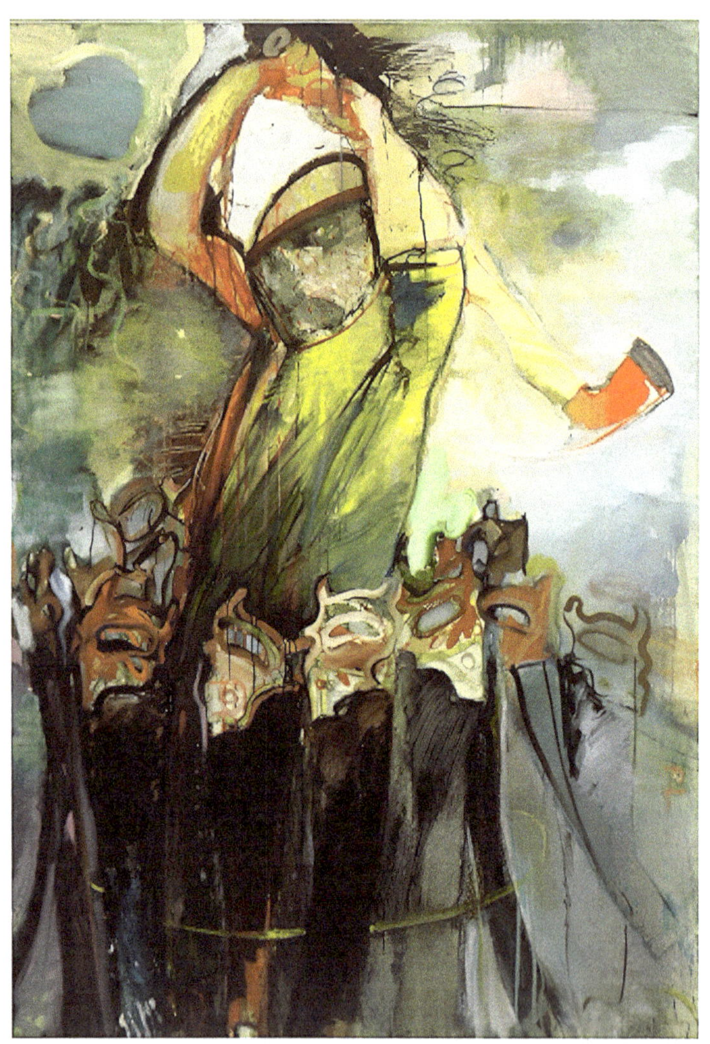

The Bee Keeper Panics, 1985-86

PETE OR ADDICTION

His head glowing with the wave of the future
That elevation of illicit duplication,
Standing beside himself threading the needle
With street risk
Not exactly adventure, but impatience
To be there………not here.

1970s

WAIT

Two snows have fallen since your departure.
My hibernating heart seeks a narrow bed
To bury dreams, like secret walnuts
Locked in perfect embrace.

Kisses darting from your smiling eyes
Span a lifetime to fuel within
The stove of memory, sparks dormant
In the body over years

Until the Spring thaws take my cover,
Break my shell, a warm bud to your touch
Making lite this short, single Winter's
Wait.

2008

LIGHT

This is a thought that grows
More leafy with each moist day
A feeling….that flows through the eyes
When they make sustained contact

Where does it begin?   The light of God
Penetrating the roots of this old tree
Into earth generations ago
Now surfacing in the iris of your eyes
Opening out like lotus petals
Breaking water surface
Finding light.

2011

POEM: CALL IT BREAKFAST

I boiled the beets
    As we stoked the fire
With your hunger
    And my red stained fingers
Touching like desire still warm
    We peeled the earthy skin
From purple flesh
    And we ate

1985

MOLTON BROWN LONDON HAND SOAP
(FOR JACKIE)

The fragrance opens
A path through the dull morning
Mind fog
To her
And a smaller
Room that could not
Contain the joy
Of generosity so shared
It permeated this bottle
To bless my day.

2011

MEDITATION ON OCTOBER MORNING GLORY

Teach me
In opaque times
My eye obscured
And need occurs

Look to the blossomed
South wall and sun's
Transparent reach
Time turned in trust
To open

Shot through white star
Ultramarine and cerise
Visions teach
Reach and release.

2010

LIGHT
(THE CARPENTER OF)

God's glue
	gathered at this jointing
Souls touched by light
	expand....dovetail
Clamping out our excess fear

By this light held
	in marvelous union
We celebrate each day
	the wedding.

1980

FULL

Sunday the giant tongue of God
    envelopes me whole as it licks
This slope of earth into warm
    moist run of blessed sensation
In particular along my nose ridge
    up into eyeball socket as you
Used to do when time forgave
    and fullness ruled

1984

FLIGHT THOUGHTS

On the window
Cruising at 34,000 feet it occurs
Some people like to close their eyes
I like to watch.

Tho flying's no longer optional
Free fall is…suicide explodes the Minnesota snow
Leaving eyeball craters in your lakes
Moving southward I remember as a kid
Poking holes in spring ice to watch
With rapture tadpoles murky movement.

1995

DAFFODIL OR ENTER YELLOW LOVE

We thought you would never come.
        Waiting, we ate
Put on a little weight and,

Hunkered down under snowboy's still,
        white watchful forecast.
We lasted through March's chill,

Until came, dame April's daffodil
        asking, may I? Wee croqui are shy
Not you, your swell yellow flies
        to flounce atop the well,
                        and enter through the eyes.

2005

CONFESSION OF THE TRICK RIDER

I ride a cruel horse named power
While chimeras of self inflate the tent.
He hates the ring my horse.
Our trick is transparent,
Still it penetrates the fearful spectator
While angry hooves transpose
To gifts of artifice, music, a bouquet verite,
From thickening air I yearn
To feel the thrill.... hot breath and equine bounce.
To stay the ring,
Maintain the tent,
Before death lays all things bare.

2010

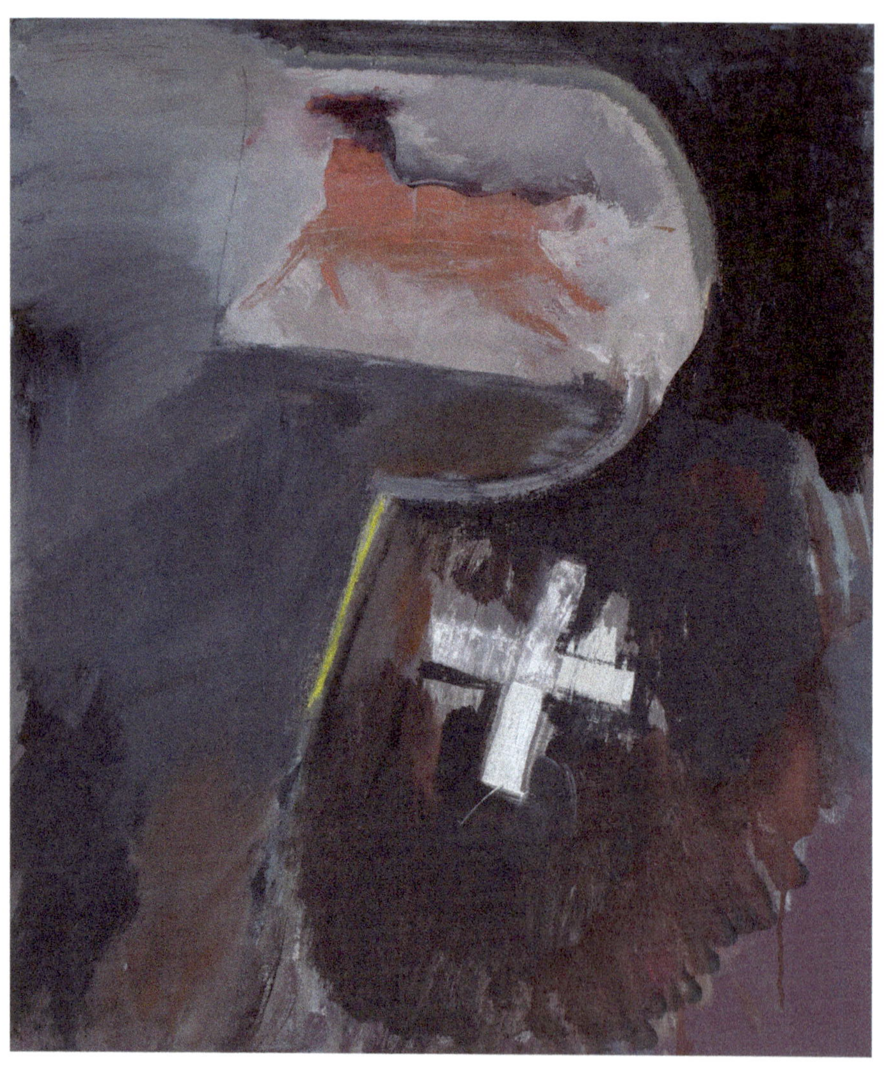

Fugitive, 2017

TO THE HEALING LIGHT
(FOR JAMES BALDWIN)

We fugitives in flight,
The anchor knot undone
To visions of safe haven.

By twins conjoined,
A light glimpsed through the bruised
Bloodshot eye of north star,
Mind bridge to freedom uncrossed.

We have trod that path
In rear view mirror and still,
So far to go, tracking true selfhood
In the long night of contradiction.

With glaring Christian cross,
Like a dirty Band-Aid, wound in need of healing light.

Expose the wound, Unseal the tombs,
To count the brothers lost.

2020

RAISING RACIST

The air surrounds
        Particles of matter impelled
This inherited disease percolates,
        Inseminates,
In youth a stagnant grip.

This fool's gold of superiority
        Takes root
Language tainted in climes
        Of light adored/then distorted.
We push this burden down the road.

2021

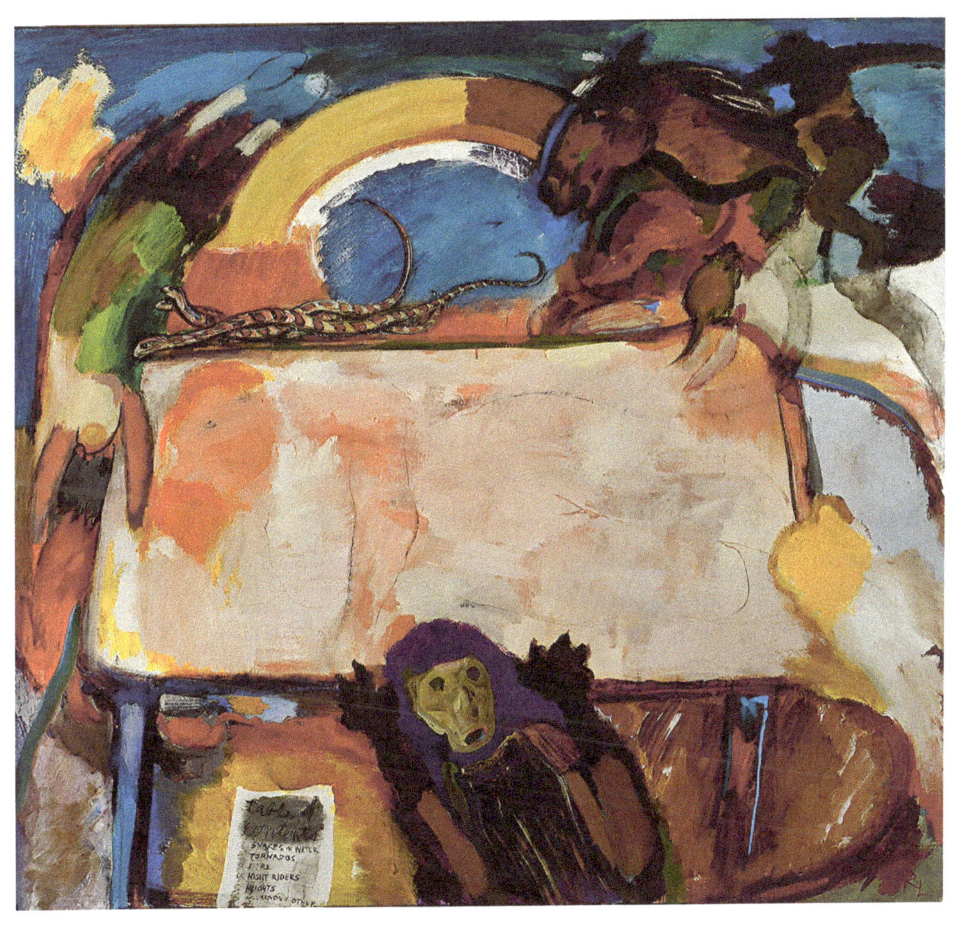

Table of Contents, 2011

TABLES OF CONTENTS

Kitchen cutting table which knows the magic knife.
The face of loss emerging from the blue table of night.
The red ground, transfer station swallowing emotional leftovers.
Body of your fears projected on the midwest water table.
The calendar, diurnal table of fleeting days and restless nights.
The work table, a random strew of concentrated casualties.

Words and figures, ghosts burnished into desk top where
We try to number and decipher the meaning of our lives.
Last, not least, the game table of distractions, parallel lines
Enclosing symbolic moves…the feints and hooks,
The yearning hoop just out of reach.

2011

STEEPLETOP
(FOR EDNA)

At the crest of a small Berkshire mountain
        The blue jays congregate
Where green gates open to the garden
        A spring fed pool for swimming,
A circled ring for dance, the picnic table
        Ample with produce fresh from the field,
A stocked wine rack over rustic bar.

Beyond the garden, surrounded by woods
        A small rough cabin, one chair, a table
For solitary work, nothing else.

For one month I inhabit this sacred spot
        Dedicated to work and pleasure, feeling
Your sharp tounged spirit rising
        Like that jay, momentarily trapped in chicken wire.

1990s

BLUE JAY IN WINTER

Pine branch, snow weighted, salted wings
That soggy yearning to have oneness in my pocket
My ego camera ready for that momentary flash of truth
Caught dilemma, despairing, ashamed of my desire
To trap red handed this accumulated life.

I spring the jaws
Undermine the dam
Scare the crow.
The shutter trips,

How to recycle the sun on melting snow, the wind, the wing.
Each well beyond control, yet left with longing.

1990s

LINE
(TO MY DRAWING STUDENTS)

The most cunning invention
Of man or woman,   line
Turning into its self,   the wheel was easy
But snapping line's whip
To capture language took some doing.

Life line gave us salvation,
Utility lines brought us voices,
Streamlined frees us from the past,
While the property line sprouts fences.

Straight from here to there
The vector line slices distance,
While illusion wanders far beyond reality
Searching for the line between.

1999

BREATHING WINGS

At window, work stopped, I saw
Amid the swirling down of maple leaves
One circle to soar again and again.
A monarch butterfly it was that stayed
To grace my blue decked morning coffee.
He/she landed etched in black on orange
To focus on the remaining impatience
As some Zen slap to capture moment,
Pulling me from inside....out.

2010

LESSONS WITH ELIZABETH IN MEETING

Large braid of marriage
Teaches in time
Love one's self first

Freeing delight in the other
Most achieved in presence
Shared, not possessed.

Silence leads to now
Prescient gentle breeze
Soul's empty tank imparted

The choice of yes
In time of dark
A self fulfilling spark

Empathy's ladder opens
Vistas with each rung
Exposing songs of union sung

2022

JOY

Two squirrels
Acrobats by trade
These two do the tight rope dash
Across the power line, effortlessly

What luck being there at the window
To catch this small drama of territory
Or was it amorousness or simple
Pleasure at being alive and capable of such daring.

But it was grace not luck…to feel the spark ignite
The moment with laughter in such solitary times
The joy you knew I needed
Lover, friend.

2021

HOME HINGE

A teacher said, regret only one thing
The failure of socialism.
The caring navel of community
Cast asunder, leads to famine despair and plunder,
Nothing good comes of greed
So oil the pin of connection and lubricate
The seed in ruddy loam, that we might celebrate
The rightful sharing,
this beneficent home.

2022

FLOSS TREE BLOSSOMS

Excess bursts of glory…silent,
fall into our lap,
entering the eye as Yates informs
love does.

My pregnant eye leaps
to possess this epiphany,
this moment of art's lust
fades like Henri's foot print in the sand
turns into faded monument,
this fleeting fall of beauty,
nature's bribe and plea.

let it go. Love does not possess.

2020

EXCAVATION OF THE EXQUISITE CORPSE

In this life we are always
        Dancing on hot coals
To assuage the rumblings
        Of fluids in the belly
While the circuitry of the busy brain
        Plays hide and seek with the soul

2014

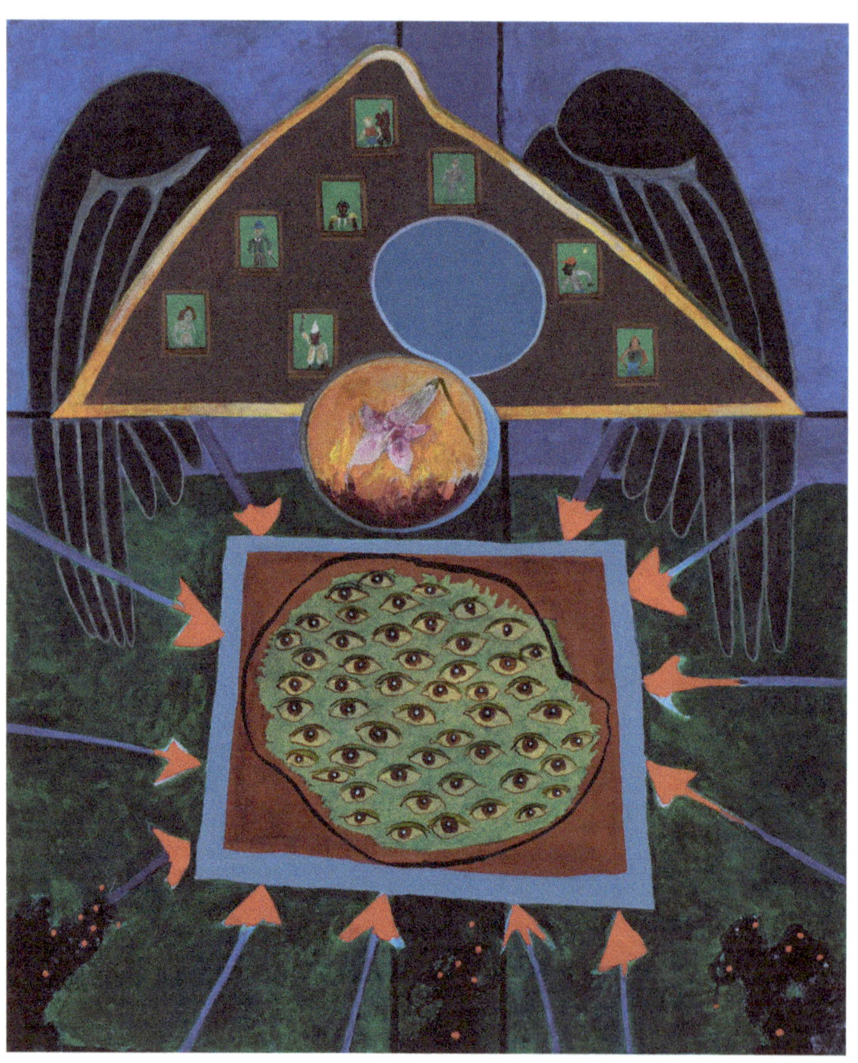

Iron Mountain/Eye of God, 2019

PRAYER (FOR HILDEGARD AUF BINGEN)

Open my eyes, my ears, my innermost soul
To the power and beauty of ongoing revelation,
The generosity of spirit….the infinite renewal of opportunity
To feel love and to love in return.
Praise be for oceans, fog, rocks and grasses,
The small and large creatures,
Therein truth speaks to us
In the present moment of our need.

2019

BIRTHMARK

In space squashed by emotion
The body floats….slow motion
In thin air…no light…no shadow
Still …I see a navel

2015

RUFOUS SIDED TOWHEE

(FOR TROSIE 2022)

An eye
For the birds of the coastal flyway
Those twenty years in Maine
Removed by circumstances to urban California
Grew dull by doves and ubiquitous grays
A noisy species unidentified in mufti.

Eureka!
A rufus sided towhee, a brash and manly male,
My first, held in pointed profile long minutes
Eight feet away, in perfect confidence
Red epaulette and blazing black eye
Staccato white notes on black tail,
Soft beige to white breast and belly.

The Audubon field guide you gave me….# 384 a perfect match
Of stunning grace the day transformed.
A nail given by god
On which to hang my hopes.

2022

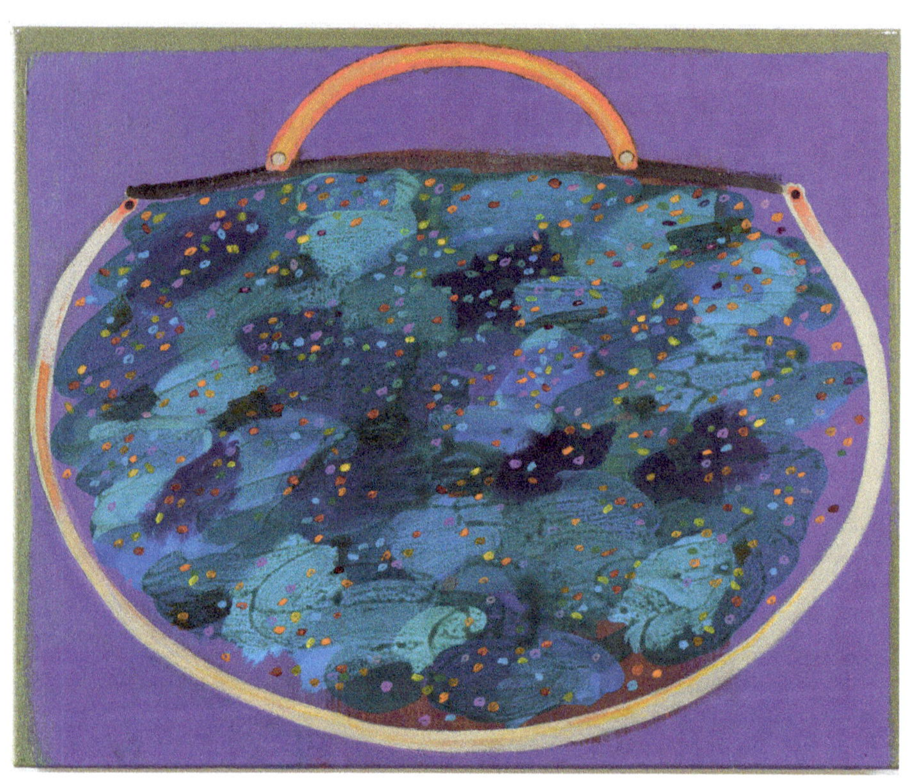

Purse of Plenty, 2021

THANKS

In gratitude I come, opened and childlike,
Lord, God
Source of all life, beauty and mystery
Enfold me in the light and water of your goodness,
The fertile soil, that I, a tiny seed, might grow
Worthy of your harvest.

2021

OPEN PRAYER

Open me o' lord
Enter and break me open
Suffer the extremes
This world of pain and pleasure
Thereby find the simple child's mind
In joyful return to your cosmic fold

2020

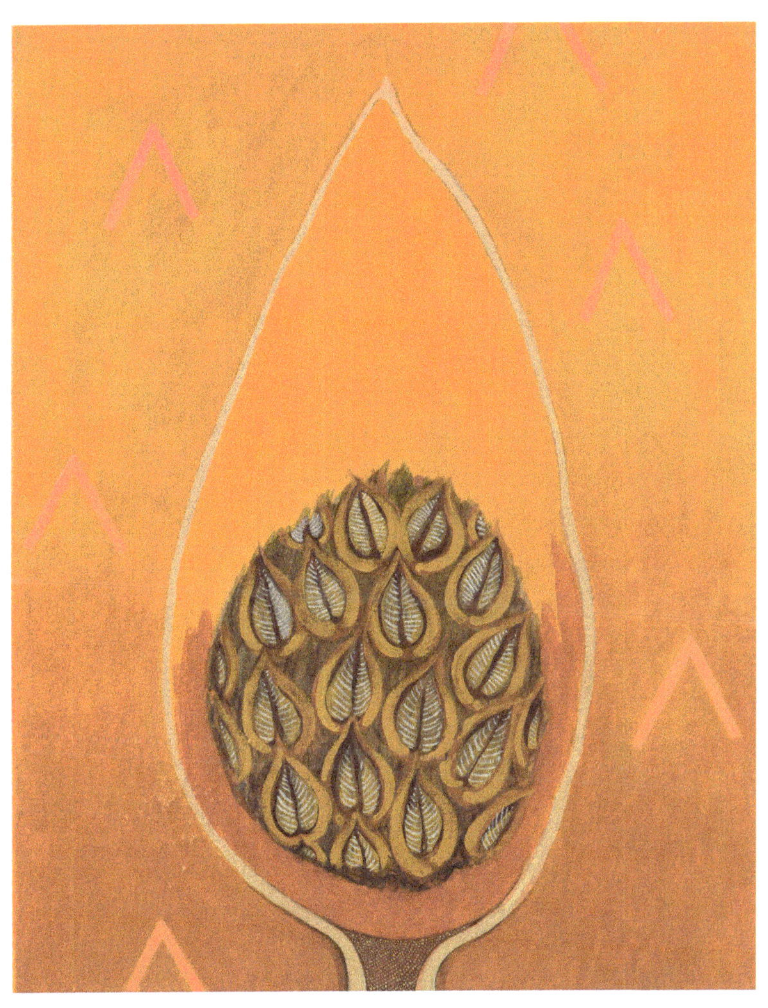

Seed in Flame, 2021

PURSE OF PLENTY

Give us this day
        The burning bush
Hearts aflame with seed
        In earth's flow
Each seed of god
        Fulfilled in giving

Purse of plenty heart's disperse
        Knowing our need bespoken
In every tongue that
        Souls have sung us
            Love among us
                        Love among us

2021

RELIQUARY : FOR MERTON TOUNGE IN CHEEK

If artists are saints, as you have argued
We might profit in exhumation and parts recycle
After all that Saint Theresa has donated
To mankind's moral good in uplift
We painters might reap the benefit
In parts revered.. reinstated to usefulness no less,
We daubers might grab hold an eyelash
Fra Angelico no longer needs
Any small thing from those angels of Sienna.
Better yet an eyeball of incomparable Velasquez, what vision hath it wrought.
Great Goya's little pinkie could raise a dust of monstrous fear.
Van Gogh, truly a saint in life without peer
would surely not with hold remaining ear.
Enterred at Pere Lachaise, Modigliani's passion no longer in need of foreskin.
And with lock of Pablo's erotic ego inspired hair combined... What a knockout!
And in the Bronx, majestic Mondrian lies waiting. Even
His big toe would know rhythms to keep alive the cerebral dance of life.

2023

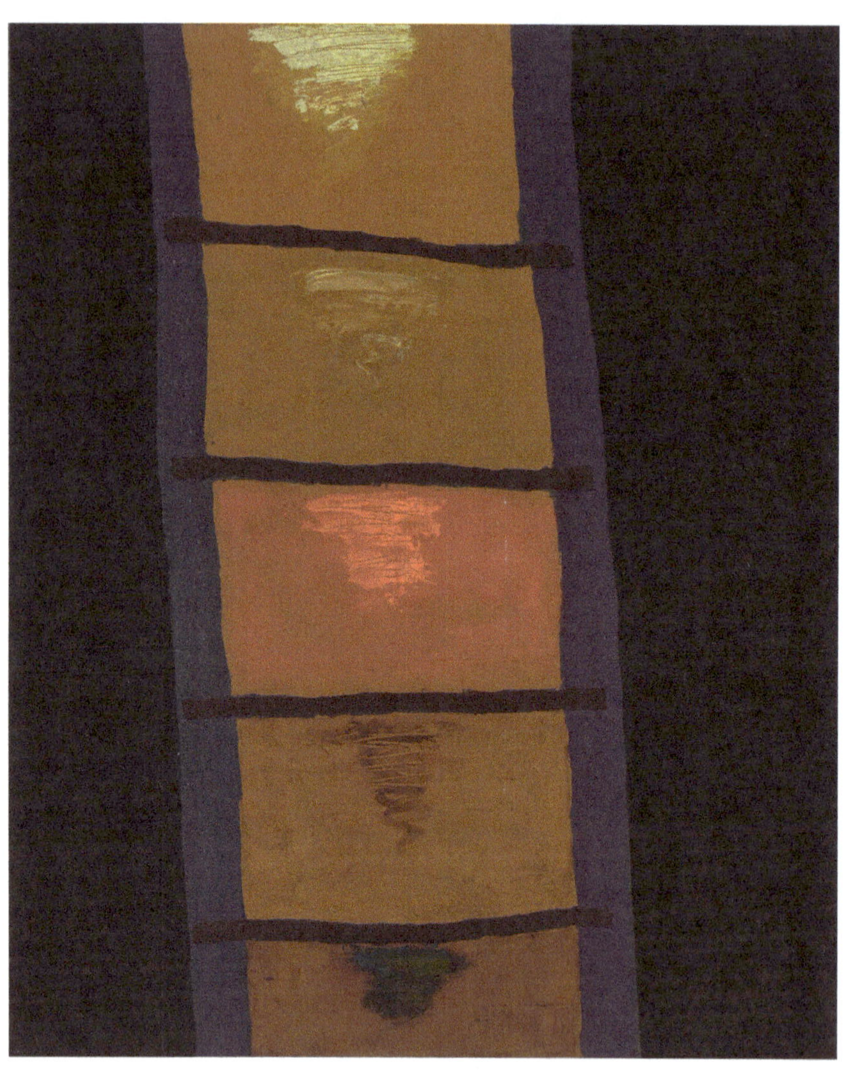

John’s Ladder, 2019

FISH LADDER

Born of the sea
I yearn for my return
Envelopment that smooths the skin
Of Mortal disrepair.

And to that end I climb the ladder
Day by day, shedding scales
Along the way.

If by chance we touch in that rush,
A precious sharing, moist sustaining moments,
Not driven by fame, but love, the undimmed desire
Of rebirth and being.

What privilege, that God-love we aspire to,
Sustaining those beyond the dam,
Scale-less and perfect in soft new skin
We share a constant Light.

2023

ABOUT THE AUTHOR

Richard Brown Lethem (b. 1932) has been living and thinking in paint on canvas since the 1950s, with results that have been categorized, more or less aptly, as abstraction, expressionism, figuration, social realism, surrealism, and allegory. Now in his 90s, Lethem's imagery has become unified and direct, often consisting of a central form derived from nature, yet distilled, by the visionary pressure of his attention, into symbols seemingly directly drawn from his psychic landscape, and beamed into that of the viewer. If this is an example of "late style," it is one defiantly uninterested in a modest contemplation of mortality; instead, the painter's wisdom exalts an embrace of color and sensuality, and traces the joyous mystery of our consistent presence as neighboring bodies in a shared field of space. He has written poetry since the 1950s to the present.

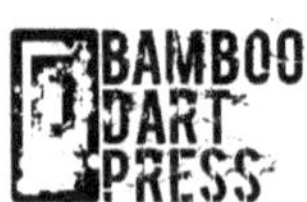

112 N. Harvard Ave. #65
Claremont, CA 91711

chapbooks@bamboodartpress.com

www.bamboodartpress.com

www.ingramcontent.com/pod-product-compliance
Lightning Source LLC
LaVergne TN
LVHW080333110826
845155LV00024B/152